WITHDRAWN

The Library of Author Biographies

Louis Sachar

The Library of Author Biographies

Louis Sachar

Meg Greene

The Rosen Publishing Group, Inc., New York

For Abbie

Published in 2004 by The Rosen Publishing Group, Inc.
29 East 21st Street, New York, NY 10010

Library of Congress Cataloging-in-Publication Data

Greene, Meg.
Louis Sachar / Meg Greene. — 1st ed.
p. cm. — (The library of author biographies)
Summary: Discusses life and work of the popular children's author, including his writing process and methods, inspirations, a critical discussion of his books, biographical timeline, and awards.
Includes bibliographical references (p.) and index.
ISBN 0-8239-4017-9 (library binding)
1. Sachar, Louis, 1954– —Juvenile literature. 2. Authors, American—20th century—Biography—Juvenile literature. 3. Children's stories, American—History and criticism— Juvenile literature. [1. Sachar, Louis, 1954– . 2. Authors, American. 3. Authorship.] I. Title. II. Series.
PS3569.A226Z67 2004
813'.54—dc21

NOV 0 2 2004

2002154252

Manufactured in the United States of America

Excerpt from *The Boy Who Lost His Face* by Louis Sachar, copyright © 1989 by Louis Sachar. Used by permission of Random House Children's Books, a division of Random House, Inc.

Excerpt from "People in the News: Louis Sachar," copyright © 1999 *U.S. News & World Report*, L.P. Reprinted with permission.

Excerpt from *There's a Boy in The Girls' Bathroom* by Louis Sachar, copyright © 1987 by Louis Sachar. Used by permission of Random House Children's Books, a division of Random House, Inc.

Table of Contents

Introduction:
Meet Louis Sachar

An elementary school thirty stories high. A story about a school bully told from the bully's point of view. A secret club known as Pig City. A nine-year-old redhead accused of picking his nose. At first glance, these might seem like unlikely subjects for stories. But not for Louis Sachar (pronounced SACK-er), who has used all of these ideas in his books for young readers.

Since 1978, Sachar has produced a diverse and popular body of work—twenty-one books to date—that has earned him fans among kids and adults. Many of his books, such as *Sideways Stories from Wayside School* (1978), *Dogs Don't Tell Jokes* (1991), and *There's a Boy in the Girls' Bathroom* (1987), appear on library and school reading lists throughout the United States. Even the most skeptical readers find themselves drawn into Sachar's sometimes silly and always offbeat world. Louis Sachar's novels, which are often praised for their humorous but realistic depiction of characters' feelings and relationships, are known for accurately charting the bumpy road to young adulthood.

Sachar credits his decision to become a writer to his older brother, Andy. When Sachar won the Newbery Medal (the highest award given for children's literature in the United States) in 1999 for *Holes*, he talked about the importance of Andy's influence on him in his acceptance speech. He said, "I'd always looked up [to] and tried to emulate [imitate] my older brother. Andy has had more of an influence on my tastes and my outlook than anyone. If he had been the type of person who had gone to business school and went to work for a big-eight accounting firm, I doubt I would be here today."[1]

Much of Sachar's success as an author lies in his refusal to underestimate the intelligence of his readers. His ability to write for kids, he explains, comes from reading books for adults. Kurt Vonnegut's *Hocus Pocus* (1990) and William

Goldman's *Princess Bride* (1987), for example, were important influences on *Holes*. "I like the way the opening chapters were sort of short and jumpy," Sachar recalls, "and how they led into the story . . . And *The Princess Bride* had these colorful characters and this bizarre setting, and that's sort of like *Holes*."[2]

Sachar believes that writing for kids is not all that different from writing for adults. Frances Foster, Sachar's editor at Farrar, Straus and Giroux, a publishing company in New York City, agrees. In an interview about Sachar, Foster said, "There's this . . . view that places children's literature below the literature written for adults. But when you think back through the ages, of what has been published for children, the really classic books have all had very high standards of plot and structure and characterization."[3]

According to Sachar's wife, Carla, there is another reason why his books are so popular. She says:

> All of us who enjoy reading his books wonder just how he is still able to tell stories from a kid's point of view and be so on the mark with children's feelings and attitudes. He vows that his characters are not based on himself or anyone he knew as a child, but once you know

him, you can see a bit of him in everyone he creates. The situations he puts his characters in are so everyday that adults can remember being there.[4]

As a result of his uncanny ability to penetrate the minds and hearts of young people, Sachar has emerged as one of the most popular children's writers of the last two decades. For his novel *Holes*—a story about a family curse, a juvenile detention center, and an unlikely hero named Stanley Yelnats—Sachar not only won the Newbery Medal in 1999, but he also won the prestigious National Book Award in 1998. And in doing so, he made history. He is the first author ever to win both awards for the same book.

Even though Sachar always wanted to write, he knew how difficult it was to get a book published. Children's writers in particular have a hard time breaking into the business. Sachar also knew that even if he were fortunate enough to see his stories in print, he might not be able to support himself and his family with his writing. For a short period, Sachar worked part-time as an attorney while trying to get his writing career off the ground. With the publication of his first book in 1978, *Sideways Stories from Wayside School*, Sachar began to gather an audience.

Frances Foster, Sachar's editor at Farrar, Straus and Giroux, compares his success to that of Roald Dahl, the well-known and beloved author of *Charlie and the Chocolate Factory* (1964) and *James and the Giant Peach* (1961). "Louis was discovered by the children who loved his books, like the Wayside School stories," Foster says. "There are books [that] adults discover and push onto kids—this was completely the other way around."[5] In fact, Sachar's popularity with kids brought him to the notice of parents, teachers, librarians, and booksellers, and that popularity has translated into success.

Today, Sachar's books have become best-sellers the world over, appearing in approximately twenty countries. About this international success, Sachar admits, "It's fun to get these books published in different languages, even though I can't read them!"[6]

According to Carla Sachar, there is another secret to Louis's success. In a piece written for *The Horn Book Magazine*, she described what she thought made her husband successful at writing for children: "Louis is a kid at heart. He loves playing games, being outside, and not working. (He doesn't consider writing 'work.') Children who read his books have either been through similar situations, hoped they would never go through anything like it, or have witnessed someone else living through it. His work crosses the boundaries of age and is enjoyed by young and old alike."[7]

1 "Louis the Yard Teacher"

Born on March 20, 1954, in East Meadow, New York, Louis Sachar is the second son of Robert J. Sachar, a salesman, and Ruth Raybin Sachar, a real estate broker. He also has an older brother, Andy. When young Louis was nine, his family moved to Tustin, located in Orange County, California. During the early 1960s, Tustin was filled with plenty of orange groves, which Sachar remembers fondly to this day. "We cut through the orange groves on the way to school," he says, "and had orange fights on the way home. Now, sadly, most of the groves have been paved over and replaced with fast-food restaurants, offices, and housing developments."[1]

Of his experiences attending Barnum Woods School in East Meadow and then Red Hill School in Tustin, Sachar recalls that "nothing especially traumatic" happened to him. For the most part, he enjoyed school, got good grades, liked math, and played Little League baseball. Sachar also remembers having "a really mean" fifth-grade teacher. "She just seemed to pick on me,"[2] he recalls. In the sixth grade, when students misbehaved, the teacher made them copy pages out of the dictionary as a punishment. Sachar never forgot that punishment and would later put it to use in *Sixth Grade Secrets* (1987).

Writer to Be?

Sachar learned to write by reading. E. B. White, the author of the classic children's book *Charlotte's Web* (1952), was one of Sachar's favorite writers. In fact, Sachar credits White with influencing his own writing. In one interview, he explained, "My favorite authors became my heroes, and I wanted to be like them."[3] Not until high school, though, did Sachar begin to enjoy reading on a deeper level. A bit of a teenage rebel, he wore his hair long despite reprimands and instructions to cut it. Of his high school years, Sachar remembers, "[My] parents fortunately were very understanding and gave me a lot of leeway . . ."[4]

Sachar first tried his hand at writing in high school. He wrote a story called "Apple Power," which was about a mean teacher named Mrs. Gorf, who turned her students into apples. "I wrote the first Mrs. Gorf story as an assignment in a creative writing class in high school," Sachar notes. "And my teacher didn't like it. In fact, she thought I hadn't taken the assignment seriously. But I always thought it was a good story."[5] The students at an elementary school (where Sachar later worked as a teacher's aide while attending college) also liked the story. In fact, the positive response from the students, Sachar notes, "made me think I might be a writer, or write longer stories."[6]

In 1972, eighteen-year-old Louis Sachar headed back east to attend Antioch College in Ohio. When his father died during his freshman year, he returned to California to be with his mother. Then Sachar decided to take a semester off before returning to school. To make money, he found a job as a door-to-door salesman. As Sachar recalls, "For three months I worked as a Fuller Brush Man [a leading manufacturer of cleaning supplies, brushes, and brooms] and I was great at it. My employers couldn't understand how I could possibly want to go back to college when I had such a great career ahead of me selling brushes."[7]

The next fall, however, Sachar was back at college, but because he had decided to stay closer to home, he enrolled at the University of California at Berkeley, where he majored in economics. Sachar's interest in becoming a writer had not diminished. Besides his required classes, he signed up for some creative writing courses. He read everything he could, though he disliked many of his English classes because, as he says, the instructors analyzed "the books to death."[8]

At one point, Sachar decided to study Russian. As he remembers, "I developed a particular interest in Russian literature and somehow got the rather ridiculously ambitious notion to learn the language and read my favorite authors in the original."[9] Despite his good intentions, Sachar soon found that Russian was not for him. "After taking over a year of Russian," he later said in an interview, "I realized it was still Greek to me. A week into the semester I dropped out . . . and tried to figure out what other class I should take instead."[10]

The Yard Teacher

It was by accident that Sachar found the answer to what he should take instead of Russian. One day, an elementary school girl was handing out leaflets on campus that read: "Help. We need teacher's aides at our school. Earn three units of credit."[11] As a teacher's aide, Sachar could earn the exact number of credits needed to make up for the Russian language course he had dropped. In addition to that benefit, Sachar thought the job sounded easy—there was no homework to do and no classes to take. Not really thinking about what he was getting into (aside from the fact that he thought it would be pretty easygoing), Sachar signed on. In a way, it was an odd decision for him to make. Sachar had little experience with children—he had never really been around them, much less worked with them in a school setting. Even Sachar admits, "Prior to that time, I had no interest whatsoever in kids."[12]

Sachar was in for a surprise. His experience at Hillside Elementary School (where he earned his three credits for being a teacher's aide) proved to be much more than an easy way to make up for the dropped Russian course. Working as a teacher's aide, Sachar says, "turned out to be not only my favorite class, but also the most important class I took during my college career."[13] Sachar soon began spending more time with the children, and he was promoted to noontime supervisor, which meant he monitored the playground during recess. For Sachar, supervising often meant playing. And because of this, he earned the title "Louis, the Yard Teacher" from the students.

Writer at Work

As Sachar was preparing to graduate, he began writing a children's story, because, as he says, "I didn't like any of the little stories that they [the students at Hillside Elementary] were reading."[14] Influenced by Damon Runyon's *In Our Town* (1946), a book of interconnected stories, Sachar wrote his own series based on events at a school he created called Wayside.

Like Runyon, who was known for his offbeat characters, the students of Wayside were also quite unusual. (Some of the Wayside students were given names of some of the students Sachar had known at Hillside.) Included among the Wayside cast of characters is Mrs. Jewl, whom Sachar based on the real-life teacher Mrs. Jukes, who taught at Hillside Elementary and for whom Sachar had worked as a teacher's aide. Sachar even had a character named Louis the Yard Teacher in his book.

Although times had changed since he was a student in Tustin, having orange fights with his friends on their way home from school, Sachar believed that kids were still basically the same as when he was young. Because a lot of the inspiration for Wayside came from his own experiences and feelings, Sachar felt that *Sideways Stories from Wayside School* would strike a chord with elementary and middle school readers.

Sachar graduated from college in 1976 with a degree in economics. After graduation, he moved to Norwalk, Connecticut, where he worked as a shipping manager for Beldoch Industries, a manufacturer of women's sweaters. In the evenings, he wrote. After seven months, Sachar was fired from his job and decided to apply to law school. In the fall of 1977, he returned to California to study law at Hastings College of Law of the University of California at San Francisco. In the meantime, Sachar mailed the manuscript of *Sideways Stories from Wayside School* to ten publishers.

A Different Kind of School

What began as a regular semester for a first-year law student soon took a surprising turn. "My first book was accepted for publication during my first week [of law school]." This event would mark the start of a six-year struggle "over trying to decide between being an author or a lawyer,"[15] Sachar says. If the book had been a failure, his decision might have been easier. However, *Sideways Stories from Wayside School* enjoyed enough success to convince Sachar that it made sense for him to keep writing.

Sideways Stories is about a unique school—the construction workers who built the school had some trouble following directions (and that's putting it mildly), and instead of being thirty classrooms long and one story high, it's one classroom long and thirty stories high. As a result, daily life at Wayside School is anything but ordinary. In the book, each chapter focuses on a particular student or teacher. Many of the students are the pupils of

Mrs. Jewl, the school's favorite teacher, whose classroom is on the thirtieth floor.

Each of Sachar's characters possesses an unusual trait. Among them are Joe, who can't count but who somehow always manages to get the right answers, and Todd, who gets into trouble every day although he doesn't do anything wrong. Meanwhile, John can only read while standing on his head, and Sammi's favorite item of clothing is a raincoat, but he also smells bad. In one story, a student named Jason is stuck to his seat by a large wad of chewing gum. And though his teacher tries throwing ice water on him to make the gum brittle so that it can be broken, Jason remains stuck. The teacher then turns Jason's chair upside down, but that does not work either. The teacher even considers cutting Jason's pants off. Jason is finally "rescued" when, much to his dismay, he is kissed by one of the girls in his class.

Sachar also included Mrs. Gorf, the teacher from "Apple Power." Still the meanest teacher, Mrs. Gorf turns her students into apples when they do something to displease her, such as misbehave in class or not know the right answer to a question. But her students eventually turn the tables on her, and Mrs. Gorf finds herself turned into an apple. When asked how he managed to think of all the silly things that happen at Wayside School, Sachar replied, "I sit at my desk and I just try to think. It may be because the life of a writer is somewhat boring, sitting alone in a room, in front of a computer screen. It forces my mind to come up with crazy things."[16]

First Reactions

While young readers responded with enthusiasm to the weird goings-on at Wayside School, some adult critics were not as favorably impressed. Some reviewers thought that the book's story line was lacking and that the book had no focus. Others felt that the humor was forced and that the writing was pedestrian, or dull. Ultimately, though, kids loved the book, and many teachers liked it, too. Its short chapters and humorous dialogue made the book easy to read aloud in classrooms.

Even though *Sideways Stories from Wayside School* had struck a chord with children and teachers, the book was difficult to find, in part because the publisher had not distributed it very effectively. As a result, the book didn't sell many copies, and the idea of Sachar supporting himself as a writer seemed unlikely. Because of this, he continued his legal studies. Even today, after having written many successful books for kids, *Sideways Stories* is special for Sachar. "I probably had more fun writing that book than any of my others," he said in an interview, "because [writing] it was just a hobby then, and I never truly expected to be published."[17]

In 1980, at the age of twenty-six, Sachar earned his law degree and prepared to take the bar exam, a test that law students must pass after they graduate in order to practice law. Sachar stayed up all night waiting for the results. He passed, but he was not excited about becoming a lawyer. All he wanted to do was write children's books.

In the end, Sachar compromised. He worked part-time as a lawyer, which allowed him the freedom he needed to write. Sachar usually wrote in the mornings and practiced law in the afternoons. The transition wasn't easy. "The hardest part," he says, "was putting on a suit and tie at one o'clock in the afternoon and going to a deposition after a somewhat bohemian morning."[18] At the same time, Sachar "stopped agonizing over the decision [of writing for children or practicing law] and realized that it had already been made."[19] For a while, Sachar balanced his career as a lawyer and his career as a writer, until at last an opportunity came along that enabled him to choose the one he most loved.

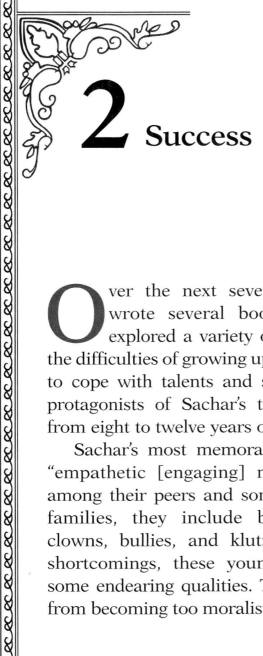

2 Success

O ver the next several years, Sachar wrote several books in which he explored a variety of themes, such as the difficulties of growing up and learning how to cope with talents and shortcomings. The protagonists of Sachar's tales range in age from eight to twelve years old.

Sachar's most memorable characters are "empathetic [engaging] misfits."[1] Outcasts among their peers and sometimes their own families, they include bookworms, class clowns, bullies, and klutzes. Despite their shortcomings, these young people possess some endearing qualities. To keep the stories from becoming too moralistic, Sachar injected his silly and offbeat brand of humor, which left adults scratching their heads and children howling with laughter.

Growing Pains

In 1981, Sachar published his second book, *Johnny's in the Basement*. The main character, Johnny Laxatayl, spends most of his time in the basement where his parents won't bother him. In creating Johnny's last name, Sachar drew on his love of puns. "Laxatayl" is a play on the phrase "lacks a tail," and it refers to Johnny's resemblance to a neighborhood dog named Popover.

Johnny's claim to fame is his amazing bottle cap collection. His world has changed since he has turned eleven, and the way Johnny sees it, the changes are not for the better. For his birthday, he receives presents more fitting for an adult, such as socks and underwear. Worst of all, he gets social-dancing lessons. Meanwhile, his parents have decided that it's time for him to grow up and start doing such chores as washing the dishes and taking out the trash. He doesn't think growing up is much fun, until one day at dancing school, he meets Valerie Plum. She hates dancing school even more than Johnny does, and the two become friends.

Johnny's parents have also made it clear that they expect him to sell off his collection of bottle caps. Johnny reluctantly agrees and receives $86.33 for his treasures. Johnny and Valerie spend all the money on things that mean nothing to them. In this way, Johnny shows his contempt for his parents' decision to make him get rid of his most prized possession.

Johnny's in the Basement is more realistic than *Sideways Stories from Wayside School*. Like many kids, Johnny learns that adults are not always right, that they make mistakes, and that sometimes kids may have a better grasp on what's important in life.

Sachar included situations in *Johnny's in the Basement* that some adults found troubling. For example, in the book, Johnny and his friends, Valerie and Donald, try smoking cigarettes. When asked why he included an episode that depicted a health risk, especially in light of campaigns to persuade kids not to smoke, Sachar replied, "When I was growing up, kids were very curious about cigarettes. We knew they were bad for us, but they didn't have the same sort of stigma as they have today. And so, kids would often experiment and try them. So, Donald experiments and tries cigarettes, as do Johnny and Valerie. But they're awful. It wasn't meant to encourage kids but to discourage them from trying cigarettes."[2]

The scene did not hurt sales. *Johnny's in the Basement* became a best-seller, earning Sachar praise from critics as well as a growing number of fans.

A Special Visit

From a boy who collects bottle caps, Sachar turned to Angeline Persopolis, an eight-year-old with a high IQ who is the main protagonist in *Someday Angeline*, which was published in 1983. Angeline's intelligence is a mixed blessing. It makes her an object of torment for her class-mates, and even her teacher thinks she is a nuisance. To make matters worse, her father, a widower, does not know what to make of his bright and talented daughter. With the help of her friend Gary "Goon" Boone and a sympathetic teacher, Miss Turbone, Angeline learns how to be happy being herself. While some critics found the story uneven in its characterizations, others praised the themes of hope and acceptance that it exemplifies.

By the time *Someday Angeline* was published, Sachar was receiving fan letters from kids all over the United States. He says, "The first book [*Sideways Stories from Wayside School*] really hit in Texas . . . I got lots of mail from kids in Houston, Dallas, all over."[3] Some of his biggest fans were the students at Davis Elementary School in Plano, who wrote to him regularly. They wanted him to visit their school. "Some of the girls had written things like, 'Our cute, single teacher thinks you're really great!'"[4] Sachar finally accepted the invitation. He did think their teacher was very nice, but he found that he liked the school counselor, Carla Askew, even better. On May 26, 1985, Louis and Carla were married and moved into a small one-bedroom apartment in San Francisco.

Carla knew her husband wanted to quit practicing law and write full-time. In *The Horn Book Magazine*, a well-respected magazine that discusses children's literature, she described her husband's struggle:

> When I met Louis, he was already a published author, had just passed the California bar exam, and was preparing his first court case. I learned very quickly that he had mixed feelings about what he really wanted to do

with his life. He had just spent a lot of time and effort earning his law degree and knew he could probably support himself doing law work. He had also had the good fortune of having his first two books accepted for publication. Common sense told him he should proceed with his career as an attorney, but his heart pushed him to keep writing. Thank goodness his heart won the battle.[5]

Not long after he met Carla, Louis Sachar decided to quit practicing law and to write full-time. After they married, Louis worked on his next book while Carla was at school. When not writing, he answered the many letters he received from children. Even during the summer when Carla was not teaching, she left their tiny apartment so that Louis could work undisturbed. Carla believed deeply in her husband's talent and never once suggested that he go back to practicing law.

Portrait of a Bully

Louis Sachar's fourth book took him longer to write than his previous works. To complicate matters, he had trouble finding a publisher. Regardless of these difficulties, many critics agree that *There's a Boy in the Girls' Bathroom* (1987) is one of Sachar's best books. The story is about the transformation of the main character, Bradley Chalker, from a bully into a confident boy. In an interesting twist, Sachar tells Bradley's story from his point of view rather than that of his victims. Sachar denies that he drew from personal experience in his portrait of Bradley, about whom a critic noted, "Sachar gives his reader the poignant and frequently unsettling opportunity to look through the eyes of a student whom every teacher dreads to see— a child to whom success, even if it were possible, would be terrifying."[6]

Bradley Chalker is bright and imaginative. He is also the oldest student in the fifth-grade class at Red Hill School, and he has earned a reputation for being a liar and a bully. Early on in the book, Sachar establishes Bradley's complete isolation from his classmates and his teacher:

> Bradley Chalker sat at his desk in the back of the room—last seat, last row. No one sat at the desk next to him or at the one in front of him. He was an island.
>
> If he could have, he would have sat in the closet. Then he could shut the door so he wouldn't have to listen to Mrs. Ebbel. He

didn't think she'd mind. She'd probably like it better that way too. So would the rest of the class. All in all, he thought everyone would be much happier if he sat in the closet, but unfortunately, his desk didn't fit.[7]

When a new student, Jeff Fishkin, tries to befriend Bradley, Bradley is cruel to him:

"Hey, Bradley, wait up!" somebody called after him.

Startled, he turned around.

Jeff, the new kid, hurried alongside him. "Hi," said Jeff.

Bradley stared at him in amazement.

Jeff smiled. "I don't mind sitting next to you," he said. "Really."

Bradley didn't know what to say.

"I have been to the White House," Jeff admitted. "If you want, I'll tell you about it."

Bradley thought a moment, then said, "Give me a dollar or I'll spit on you."[8]

Because the kids at school hate him, Bradley turns to his collection of chipped and broken pottery animals for comfort. Talking to them allows him to be all the things he cannot be with people: brave, smart, caring, and vulnerable. But Jeff Fishkin won't give up, and after mostly unpleasant encounters, the two boys gradually start to become friends.

There is another newcomer to Red Hill School, one who will play an even bigger role in Bradley's life. Carla, the new school counselor, known for the brightly colored shirts she wears, makes a point of seeking Bradley out. With her help, Bradley begins to see himself as less of a monster and more of the person he wants to be. With the support of Carla and Jeff, Bradley takes his first faltering steps toward gaining self-esteem. He begins to do his homework, and instead of holding up his failing papers for all the class to see, he treasures the gold stars his teacher hands out for good work. While the process is slow and at times painful, Bradley changes from the boy nobody liked to one who works hard at being a good friend and learning how to trust.

Sachar originally wanted the story to be told from two points of view: Bradley Chalker's and Jeff Fishkin's. His editors, however, thought the book would work better if the story was told from Bradley's point of view. This meant several rewrites for Sachar. In creating Carla Davis, the school counselor, Sachar borrowed his wife's first name and drew upon her experiences.

Another problem with the book was choosing a title. "The title is usually the last thing I think of," Sachar explains. "Although the whole time I'm writing the book, I'm trying to think of what I'll call it. But I discovered how important titles were with the success of *There's a Boy in the Girls' Bathroom*. Prior to that book, I hadn't been that successful. And that title got people to notice."[9] For some critics, the title was a bit misleading. One reviewer for the *Bulletin of the Center for Children's Books* saw the book as "funny" but "not in the flip way implied by the title, but in the slightly sad sense that touches all true comedy."[10]

Critics found much to like about *There's a Boy in the Girls' Bathroom*. One reviewer for *Kirkus Reviews* described it as the "fall and rise of Bradley Chalkers, class bully,"[11] while a review in *School Library Journal* raved that it was "unusual, witty, and satisfying."[12] Young readers once more showed their loyalty, and the book soon appeared on reading lists at libraries and schools across the United States.

There's a Boy in the Girls' Bathroom also pointed Louis Sachar in a new direction. Moving away from the silly stories that had been so successful in *Sideways Stories from Wayside School,* Sachar began delving deeply into the world of preteens and their struggles to fit in with their peers while trying to navigate the pitfalls of growing up.

3

From Middle School to Grade School

The success of *There's a Boy in the Girls' Bathroom* indicated that Sachar could address the sensitive issues that many preteens face, and the believable characters he created demonstrated his ability as a writer to capture the nuances of the middle school world. Sachar revisited the themes of acceptance and responsibility in two more books, *Sixth Grade Secrets*, published in 1987, and *The Boy Who Lost His Face*, published in 1989.

A Different Direction

In Sachar's novel *Sixth Grade Secrets*, eleven-year-old Laura Sibbie is the envy of her sixth-grade classmates. Meanwhile, one classmate, Gabriel, has a crush on her. After finding a cap at a yard sale with the words "Pig City" written on it, Laura and her friends decide to form a secret club of the same name. To ensure that no one finds out about the club, they each write down a secret, place it in a box, and agree never to talk about the club. If anyone breaks her promise, the other girls will reveal her secret to the entire school.

In the meantime, Gabriel writes a nice note to Laura in an effort to win her affection, but Sheila, a jealous classmate who likes Gabriel, intercepts the note and rewrites it. Laura reads the note (which is now mean) and vows to get even with Gabriel, and after quarreling with Laura, Gabriel creates a rival club called Monkey Town. The members of both clubs begin to play silly pranks and tricks on each other. Unfortunately, though, the contest turns nasty: Gabriel steals the box with the secrets inside and reveals them to the entire sixth-grade class, while Sheila and a friend cut off Laura's hair. Seeing how much damage the secrets and pranks have caused, Laura realizes that she and her classmates have behaved foolishly. She also learns Gabriel's true feelings about her. By the end of *Sixth Grade Secrets*, Laura has learned not to jump to hasty conclusions that can be hurtful.

Growing Up Is Hard to Do

In *The Boy Who Lost His Face* (1989), Sachar explores the worries and fears of middle schoolers. The main character, David Ballinger, wants to be part of the "in" crowd like his friend Scott. But David is afraid that he is too awkward to fit in. In an effort to be popular, David helps the group attack an elderly woman named Mrs. Bayfield, who, according to his new "friends," is a witch who steals people's faces. During the attack (in which David takes away Mrs. Bayfield's cane), Mrs. Bayfield puts a curse on David.

At first, David thinks that this is nonsense, but when odd things begin to happen to him, such as falling backward in his chair during class and forgetting to pull up the zipper of his pants before Spanish class, he begins to believe that she really has cursed him. After more strange things occur, David visits Mrs. Bayfield and asks her to remove the curse. He tries to explain that he didn't really take part in the attack, and he asks if he is going to be cursed for the rest of his life. "Do I have to spend my whole life wondering when my pants are going to fall down?"[1] he asks. In response, Mrs. Bayfield reminds David,

> Isn't that what life is all about? . . . We all pretend we're such important, dignified people. We become doctors or lawyers or artists. Hello. How are you? Let's have a barbecue on the Fourth of July. But really we all know that at any moment our pants might fall down.[2]

Eventually, David learns the importance of being true to himself and accepting responsibility for his actions. He redeems himself by retrieving and returning Mrs. Bayfield's cane, though not without suffering some bumps and bruises along the way. Eventually, David realizes that he is the lucky one: His true friends accept him for who he is and not for who he pretends to be, unlike Scott.

With *The Boy Who Lost His Face*, Sachar's writing moved further away from the silly and gentle humor that marked his earlier books. At the heart of this story, however, are the themes that Sachar has visited again and again: the quest for identity and acceptance and the often bumpy ride that marks the transition from childhood to adolescence. For the first time,

Sachar used mature language and situations in *The Boy Who Lost His Face*. The characters swear, and the attack on an elderly woman marked a rather violent departure for Sachar. His editors were worried. In fact, they convinced him to tone down some of the language. Speaking about his decision to incorporate profanity and his reasons for removing some of the offensive words, Sachar notes:

> Initially the book had the 'f' word in it. My editor approved it, knowing full well I don't use words indiscriminately [randomly], but right before the book was published, a consultant informed me that if I didn't take it out, I'd be killing the sales of the book, as well as hurt my other books, and possibly kill my career in the process. Every single word in my books is important to me; however, I also know that kids don't worry about individual words as much when they're reading as I do when I'm writing. Although I believed the word belonged where I had put it, I agreed to change the text, because it would not ultimately affect how readers responded to the book. I find it very interesting that what people often object to is the word itself, rather than to content. As much as I might back down and change a word, I would never consider altering the moral or political content of a story.[3]

A Return to Familiar Territory

Although Sachar continued to experiment in his writing, the combination of letters from his young fans and the difficulty he had finding a publisher for *There's a Boy in the Girls' Bathroom* convinced him to return to Wayside School for his next book. In 1989, he published *Wayside School Is Falling Down*, a sequel to *Sideways Stories from Wayside School*. In *Falling Down*, fans of the first Wayside book welcomed back the students in Mrs. Jewl's class, who participate in a variety of zany antics, including a lesson in gravity that involves Mrs. Jewl's dropping a classroom computer out a window.

Sachar explores the themes of self-awareness, identity, and popularity in *Wayside School Is Falling Down*, but this time, his treatment of these serious themes is more humorous than it was in *The Boy Who Lost His Face*. In *Falling Down*, Benjamin Nushmutt, a new student to Mrs. Jewl's class, is mistakenly introduced as another student named Mark Miller. But before Benjamin can tell Mrs. Jewl about her mistake, he has become known as Mark Miller. Benjamin discovers that this new identity allows him to act differently, and he rather enjoys the change. Ultimately, though, Benjamin renounces his alter ego and reclaims his true identity—he has learned to be comfortable with himself, and he is "proud to be in a class where nobody was strange because nobody was normal."[4]

Critics praised *Wayside School Is Falling Down*. The short chapters added to the book's appeal by making it easy for teachers to read aloud, just as they had done with the first Wayside book. Continuing with the successful Wayside School novels, Sachar published *Sideways Arithmetic from Wayside School* (1989), in which he indulged his love of mathematics by creating a collection of math puzzles. About this book, Sachar has this to say:

> While working on *There's a Boy in the Girls' Bathroom*, I wrote for about two hours every morning, and then every afternoon I made up a puzzle for the sequel to *Sideways Stories* entitled *Sideways Arithmetic from Wayside School*. Having enjoyed math so much when I was in grade school, I wanted *Sideways Arithmetic* to help kids discover that math could be fun. Unfortunately, I think a lot of kids flip through the book, see all the puzzles, and automatically assume it will be too difficult, so they don't even

attempt it. When I visit schools and put the first puzzle on the board, I ask the often lost-looking class to help solve it. Receiving little or no response, I go through it aloud, showing them step by step. When the next problem goes up on the board, kids start shouting answers.[5]

In 1995, Sachar returned to Wayside School one more time, writing *Wayside School Gets a Little Stranger*, a collection of thirty stories revolving around Mrs. Jewl's maternity leave.

By 1990, *There's a Boy in the Girls' Bathroom* had won several prizes, including the Texas Bluebonnet Award. Shortly after traveling to Texas to accept the award, the Sachars decided to leave San Francisco and move to Austin. They had recently become parents of a baby girl, Sherre, born in 1989. Luckily, having a child didn't mean that there was a lot less time to write. To make sure her husband had the quiet time he needed, Carla Sachar dropped Sherre off at the baby-sitter's before going to work. At home, Louis wrote in the mornings and answered letters or did research in the afternoons. Then before Carla and Sherre returned home, he cleaned up his materials and put the house in order.

Meet Marvin Redpost

In 1992, Sachar introduced his fans to a new character, Marvin Redpost, a red-haired nine-year-old who lives near Washington, D.C. In *Marvin Redpost: Kidnapped at Birth?* (1992), Marvin convinces himself that he is a long-lost prince who was stolen from his real parents, the king and queen of Shampoon, and was adopted by the Redpost family. In the Marvin Redpost series, Sachar reexamines the theme of identity. Directed toward younger readers, the Redpost books also explore the importance of friendship and education. Adding to the books' appeal are their short chapters filled with fast-paced dialogue and comic situations.

During the next several years, Sachar wrote a number of Redpost books. In *Marvin Redpost: Is He a Girl?* (1993), Sachar pokes fun at the stereotypical characteristics of boys and girls. He addresses social taboos in *Marvin Redpost: Why Pick on Me?* (1993), a book in which Marvin becomes an outcast after being falsely accused of picking his nose.

Sachar's book *Marvin Redpost: Alone in His Teacher's House* (1994) takes on a weightier subject—death. When his teacher asks Marvin to take care of his aging dog, Waldo, Marvin is the envy of his friends. But when Waldo dies while in Marvin's care, he is overcome by feelings of guilt and grief, even though the death was not his fault. To make matters worse, Marvin must deal with his classmates' cruel jokes and teasing about Waldo's death—one boy even tells him he could go to jail for "killing" Waldo. Meanwhile, the substitute teacher (who has no idea what has happened) is annoyed with Marvin because he's not paying attention in class.

Sachar treats the death of a beloved pet with sensitivity. Through Marvin's dealings with Waldo and his teacher, Sachar shows that Marvin is beginning to grow up. Rather than feeling sorry for himself, ultimately, Marvin is more concerned about his teacher's sadness than about defending himself against false charges.

Gary "Goon" Boone

In between working on the Marvin Redpost books, Sachar returned to coming-of-age stories. In *Dogs Don't Tell Jokes* (1991), Gary "Goon" Boone (who first appeared in *Someday Angeline*) is a compulsive joke-teller who thinks all of his jokes are hysterical. However, they aren't.

Gary, who is in the seventh grade, dreams of becoming a stand-up comic. The problem is that he is not funny. As a result, almost everyone gets tired of his jokes. When a talent show with a $100 prize is announced at school, Gary is convinced his moment has arrived. He decides to enter, but his parents have an alternate plan in mind. They promise to give him $100 if he stops telling jokes for three weeks. Gary accepts his parents' proposition only to find that not telling jokes proves to be harder than he imagined. He tries collecting baseball cards and playing football, but nothing can replace his jokes.

Eventually, with the help of an invisible friend, Mrs. Snizberry, who offers Gary helpful advice, he starts to learn the kind of hard work and practice that goes into being a comic. Ultimately, being able to tell the difference between good jokes and bad jokes forces Gary to stop hiding behind his humor, and he becomes more willing to listen to others. *Dogs Don't Tell Jokes* explores familiar thematic territory for Sachar. Gary searches for his identity and tries to discover what makes him happy. Eventually, he realizes that there is a time to joke and a time for being serious. Knowing the difference between the two is important.

By the time he published *Dogs Don't Tell Jokes*, Sachar had a reputation as one of the most talented children's writers of the 1980s and 1990s. But it was a summer trip to Maine and the hot summers of Texas that enabled Sachar to produce his greatest work.

4 *Holes*

L ouis Sachar hates the summer heat, especially the summer heat in Texas. As Carla Sachar describes it, "Often just walking out of the air-conditioned house into a summer day can take your breath away."[1] Sachar adds, "There are no breaks from the Texas summer heat. It starts, if we're lucky, in late May, and continues until almost Halloween. September and October are the worst. In July and August you expect it to be hot. That's part of the bargain. But then it just keeps going on, week after week, while you know that in other parts of the country people are enjoying crisp fall air and colorful leaves."[2]

In 1995, to get away from the oppressive summers of Austin, the Sachar family went to Maine. While there, Sachar worked on a novel for adults, a project that he had begun nearly two years earlier. The book went nowhere; the plot was thin and the characters never really developed. Once Sachar realized that it was no use to continue, he abandoned the manuscript. When he and his family returned to Austin, where the hot summer lingered, little did Sachar know, but, as Carla wrote, "Louis's loathing of this heat would be just the emotion to encourage him to write his latest book."[3]

Sachar was ready for a new challenge. As he recalls, "I had already written lots of books about kids in school. I wanted to do something completely different. I was sick of school. It was August, and the weather was hot, and I got the idea to write about a juvenile correctional facility, a boot camp for 'bad boys,' where the boys were required to dig holes, every day, under the brutal Texas sun."[4]

For the next year and a half, Sachar wrote and wrote. And from the outset, he was aware that the book he was writing was different from anything he had done before. For one thing, he always began writing with a specific character in mind. However, this time he didn't have one. Instead, he was inspired by a setting, a place that he called Camp Green Lake, even though there was no lake and nothing green anywhere in sight. He explains how the book began to unfold:

> Every day I would begin by turning on my computer and typing the word "try." This turned out to be very helpful, psychologically. *Holes* was the most ambitious book I'd ever tried to write. There were times when it seemed hopeless, when the story got so bogged down that I didn't think I could ever make it work—and this after spending two years on a novel that I'd never finished. So it was very comforting to begin each day by telling myself just to try.[5]

Sachar later admitted later that he "didn't know what was going to happen there, or even who the main character would be . . . But . . . the place seemed ripe for a story."[6] The book took off from there.

> Perhaps it was a result of the frustration of having worked two years on a novel that lacked strong characters and plot. As soon as I came up with the idea that the juvenile inmates of Camp Green Lake would be required to dig holes, almost immediately I

had the idea that there would be buried treasure somewhere out there. I decided it was buried by a famous outlaw named Kissin' Kate Barlow, although I didn't know anything about her yet, and I decided that the warden would be the granddaughter of Kate Barlow, who was using the juvenile delinquents as slave labor to look for her grandmother's buried treasure. And I made up the deadly yellow-spotted lizards, lurking somewhere out there, although I didn't know what I'd do with them yet.[7]

Stanley Yelnats and *Holes*

Holes is the story of Stanley Yelnats, an overweight kid with no friends and even less luck. He gets teased in school and lives in an apartment that smells like dirty feet. To make matters worse, Stanley suffers from a family curse that began with his great-great-grandfather, Elya Yelnats. When Stanley is wrongfully accused of stealing a pair of sneakers, he has a choice: go to jail or go to Camp Green Lake, an institution for wayward boys, where the strange philosophy of reha-bilitation is "If you take a bad boy and make him dig a hole every day in the hot sun, it will turn him into a good boy."[8] Stanley blames his latest streak of bad luck on his "no-good-dirty-rotten-pig-stealing-great-great-grandfather,"[9] whose failure to honor a promise to an old gypsy woman named Madame Zeroni began the family's history of misfortune.

A villainous female warden operates Camp Green Lake. She keeps her charges in line with fingernails that are polished with rattlesnake venom. One scratch, and the unlucky inmate is poisoned. The Warden also forces the inmates to dig holes, each one approximately 5 feet (1.5 meters) deep and 5 feet across. If the boys find anything in the course of their digging, they are to report immediately to the Warden.

When taken to the work area, Stanley sees a landscape "so full of holes and mounds that it reminded him of pictures he'd seen of the moon."[10] Day after day, as Stanley digs, he begins to wonder if in fact there isn't something buried in the sand. When Stanley does discover the truth, he unknowingly sets into motion a series of events that will fulfill his destiny, bringing the past and present together.

Sachar had two big problems writing *Holes*: "I wanted to put the background in about Stanley's great-great-grandfather, and I didn't want to just all of a sudden in the middle of the story just go, 'Okay, now here's what happened to Stanley's great-great-grandfather.'"[11] The other problem was how to keep readers interested in Stanley and the hole digging without getting repetitive: "I wanted the reader to feel what a long, miserable experience this is, digging this 5' by 5' (1.5 m x 1.5 m) hole. But how many times can you say, 'He dug his shovel back into the dirt and lifted out another shovelful?'"[12]

Sachar solved the problem by interweaving the story of Stanley at Camp Green Lake with the story of his great-great-grandfather. Added to the story line is the fact that while Stanley knows some of his family's history, the reader often finds out more before he does or even at the same time as Stanley. Sachar's use of alternating between the past and the present keeps the pace moving and readers on their toes. As each piece of the puzzle falls into place, Stanley's quest to break the family curse becomes even more important.

By connecting the two stories, Sachar shows that history repeats itself. Just like Stanley, Elya Yelnats was in the wrong place at the wrong time and, as a result, lost his entire fortune at the hands of Kissin' Kate Barlow, a ruthless

Texas outlaw who used to be a schoolteacher in Green Lake and was famous for her spiced peaches. Sachar structured Kate's and Elya's story to parallel Stanley's. Though the novel may seem a bit haphazard in the beginning, the two story lines come together to lead to a rousing climax. To unite the two story lines, Sachar incorporated a make-believe folk song, the "Pig Lullaby," which the Yelnats family sings:

> "If only, if only," the woodpecker sighs,
>
> "The bark on the tree was just a little bit softer."
>
> While the wolf waits below, hungry and lonely,
>
> He cries to the moo–oo–oon,
>
> "If only, if only."[13]

One of the most successful aspects of *Holes* comes from Sachar's use of folkloric devices such as the lullaby. As well, his repetition of themes and phrases throughout the book, such as his description of Stanley's friend, Zero ("Zero said nothing"), resonated with readers and critics alike. When Zero finally does say something, it is crucial to the story's plot.

Success!

Sachar gave the manuscript of *Holes* to his eight-year-old daughter, Sherre, to read. She pointed out the parts of the book that worked and the parts that didn't. As with *There's a Boy in the Girls' Bathroom*, Sachar had a hard time coming up with a good title. He didn't really like the proposed title, *Holes*, and thought instead of going with the one that he and Sherre liked best: *Wrong Place, Wrong Time, Wrong Kid*. In the end, though, *Holes* won out. Sachar also decided to keep Stanley's last name, explaining later that he "came up with the name Stanley Yelnats because [he] didn't feel like figuring out a last name." As he said, "I just spelled his last name backwards and figured I'd change it later. But I didn't."[14] Sachar created one of his most memorable characters in Stanley, the luckless boy whose name is a palindrome.

Based on his daughter's recommendations and his own need to revise the text, Sachar did another draft of the manuscript. In all, he wrote five drafts of *Holes* before he was satisfied enough with it to send it out. *Holes* was published in 1998. The book became a huge success with readers of all ages and received universal praise from reviewers and critics. One reviewer called it a "dazzling blend of social commentary, tall tale and magic realism," and found it to be "a wry [clever] and loopy novel."[15] It seemed that tons of young readers identified with Stanley, a fact that wasn't that surprising to Sachar, who explains:

> Stanley isn't a hero-type. He's kind of a pathetic kid who feels like he has no friends, feels like his life is cursed. And I think everyone can identify with that in one way or another. And then the fact that here he is, a kid who isn't a hero—he rises and becomes one. I think people can see themselves rising with Stanley.[16]

Holes marked another departure for Sachar. It is a much darker, much scarier, and more disturbing work than his previous efforts. Even Sachar's daughter found the character of the Warden frightening, though Sachar says he was surprised by Sherre's response. To him, the Warden—with her rattlesnake-venom fingernails —was "almost cartoonish . . . like a character in *Batman* or something."[17]

Winning the Newbery

Holes received a number of awards, including the 1998 National Book Award. However, among the biggest surprises for Sachar was the announcement in February 1999 that *Holes* had won the Newbery Medal—the highest honor a children's author can win in the United States. Sachar was "amazed" when he heard the news, and he recalled the phone call in his acceptance speech: "I was awakened by a phone call at seven o'clock in the morning on February 1 and was told the great news. I could tell I was on a speakerphone, and I knew they were eagerly awaiting my reaction. I felt I was letting everyone down by not screaming. Sorry."[18]

In June 2002, one thousand young adult readers selected *Holes* to receive the first annual Readers' Choice Award for Teen Books, presented by *Read* magazine. *Read* is a literary magazine for grades six through ten, and is published by *Weekly Reader*. The award, established in honor of *Read* magazine's fiftieth anniversary, is the first of its kind. Although there are many state awards programs that involve a student selection committee, the Readers' Choice Award is the first and only national award for which the nominees and the winners are chosen entirely by students. Competition for the award was tough and included popular children's authors such as

Christopher Paul Curtis (*The Watsons Go to Birmingham*, 1995), Richard Peck (*A Year Down Yonder*, 2000), J. K. Rowling (*Harry Potter and the Goblet of Fire*, 2000), and Jerry Spinelli (*Stargirl*, 2000).

While prestigious awards and the recognition that comes with winning them can be enjoyable, they are certainly not the most important thing in Louis Sachar's life; you can tell by what he says when questioned about his status as a recognized author. In an interview he gave after winning the Newbery, Sachar stated, "Well, I suppose it's nice to get recognition from people who matter. In a sense."[19] When an interviewer asked him if fan letters and awards from children outweigh the honor of winning national awards, Sachar replied simply, "They're both nice."[20] And whenever anyone asked about the possibility of *Holes* being made into a movie, Sachar remained unflappable, saying, "I try not to get too excited."[21]

Holes—The Movie

The actual fact of the matter is, regardless of how much he downplays his success, Sachar has good reason to be very excited. Teresa Tucker-Davies, a producer for the Chicago Pacific Entertainment

Company, came across a synopsis of *Holes* and knew immediately that she had just found her next film project. The company bought the film rights, and director Andrew Davis, who also headed Chicago Pacific Entertainment, signed on to direct. Never for a moment did Sachar think that the producers or the director would want him to write the screenplay. He believed they would hire someone with more experience. However, during one meeting, Sachar recalls, "They turned to me and said, 'How about you?'"[22]

Finding the actors proved more of a challenge than was expected. Andrew Davis admits, "It was harder on Louis than us to cast the boys—he'd lived with the characters in his head for so long." Sachar adds, "We didn't want TV commercial actors . . . We needed slightly goofy kids."[23] The cast includes Shia LaBeouf as Stanley, Sigourney Weaver as the Warden, and Henry Winkler as Stanley's father. Sachar himself has a small role as a shopkeeper in the town of Green Lake.

Working on the film version of *Holes* gave Sachar a bird's-eye view of how films are made. In an interview he gave while on the set, Sachar said, "Everyone thinks that writing a screenplay is just dialogue. But it's not. It's making things visual."

Sachar has learned a great deal from his experience: "Now that I've seen the work out here, I think I'd be better at it. I watch movies differently now."[24]

The Legacy of *Holes*

In retrospect, Sachar is unsure whether he did the best he could have done with *Holes*, although he felt good about the book when he sent it to his publisher. "I get a real clear vision at different parts of a book," he says. "I know what I'm going to do here. And then I get kind of lost. I'm always amazed when I finish a book and realize, 'Hey this is actually what I set out to do.'"[25]

Sachar has been asked countless times what theme or message he hoped to convey in *Holes*. In his acceptance speech for the Newbery Medal, he pointed out that he "didn't write the book for the purpose of teaching kids that something their great-great-grandparents did long ago might have cursed them . . ." He continued, "I included the curse only because I think most adolescents can identify with the feeling that their lives must be cursed. The book was written for the sake of the book, and nothing beyond that. If there's any lesson at all, it is that reading is fun."[26]

Sachar did tell one reporter that "the best morals kids get from any book is just the capacity to empathize with other people, to care about the characters and their feelings. So you don't have to write a preachy book to do that. You just make it a fun book with characters they care about, and they will become better people as a result."[27]

5 How Does He Do It?

ike any writer, Louis Sachar has his own writing routine. According to Carla, Louis begins every day in the same way. He showers and dresses before making his way to the kitchen, where he drinks a glass of freshly squeezed grapefruit juice, boils water for his morning cup of tea, and makes his breakfast. He then reads the morning paper, always taking time to solve the daily bridge column. Even if the Sachars have guests, the visitors soon learn that Louis doesn't chat over breakfast. As soon as he is finished eating, it's off to the study, which is located in a room above the garage, where he begins writing.

Behind a Closed Door

As soon as the door to Sachar's office is closed, it is a signal to everyone in the house that he is at work. No one is allowed into the room; the only exceptions are the family's two dogs, Lucky and Tippy, who wait outside the office door every morning for Sachar to arrive. Once inside the office, both dogs have special places to sit or sleep while their master writes. Lucky, in particular, senses that he has been given an important responsibility. According to Sachar, "He growls at my wife or my daughter if they try to enter."[1] Sometimes, when Sachar is just beginning a new book, the house will be filled with the sounds of his pinball machine (located in his office) as he takes a break to think things over.

Sachar follows a strict work regime. He writes on a computer using an old program called Wordstar, which does not require a mouse or a version of Windows to operate. Sachar discusses his method of writing:

> I write every morning. After about two hours, I can feel myself losing energy and concentration. It's best to quit when I'm still excited about what I'm writing. Then I'll be ready to go when I start the next day. I couldn't write for a longer amount of time, even if I wanted

to. Tippy has gotten used to my schedule, and after two hours she taps me with her paw, howls, barks, and otherwise lets me know it's time for her walk.[2]

Sometimes when working on a first draft, Sachar may work only forty-five minutes each day. Then he lets the draft sit for twenty-four hours and returns to it the next day. To keep the process moving along, he gives his computer files some interesting names. During the writing of *Holes* for instance, Sachar called some of his early files NowWhat and AndThen because he was unsure what would happen next as he wrote.

Sachar writes five days a week. When asked what he likes most about writing, he replied, "I think it's [the] tremendous feeling of accomplishment that I get from starting with nothing, and somehow creating a whole story and setting and characters."[3] But Sachar admits that there's also a downside to writing. This is what he has to say about what he likes the least about writing:

Most days, it just feels like I'm not accomplishing much . . . most of it just seems like a waste of time. It amazes me how after a year, all those wasted days somehow add up to nothing. Another thing I don't like is that it's a very solitary profession. I think it would be nice sometimes to go to an office and see people every day, instead of just sitting in my room.[4]

While Sachar reserves the mornings for writing, he devotes his afternoons to answering the letters he receives from young fans. As his success and fame have grown, writing a personal response to every correspondent has become harder. According to Carla, "The letters may sit in a pile on the floor across from his desk for weeks at a time, [but Louis] always takes time to personally answer all of the mail from his readers . . . Each child is important to him, so he is determined to give them all the respect they deserve."[5]

A Special Rule

There is one other important rule in the Sachar household. Sachar makes it a practice to never discuss his work in progress because, as he says, "By working on a book for a year without talking about it—even to my wife—the story keeps building inside, until it's bursting to be told and the words come pouring out when I sit down to write."[6] Sachar's daughter, Sherre, calls her father's rule "one of my dad's toughest." She and her mother might know only that her father's current project is a Marvin Redpost book or another Wayside School book. Sachar, according to Sherre, "doesn't want anyone giving him suggestions; he says it interferes with his creative process."[7]

For Carla and Sherre, the wait is worth it. When Sachar finishes a manuscript, he lets them read it. As Sherre describes it, "We both love the day when Dad says, 'OK, my book is finished. Anyone want to read it?'"[8] Sherre will tell her dad when there's something that might be hard for kids to understand, while Carla looks for errors. Sachar always wants lots of feedback at this point before he begins to rework the material.

Sachar admits he wasn't sure how having a family would affect his writing. In one interview, he stated, "When I first started writing, I spent a great deal of time alone. Solitude allowed me to think about a project at all times—even when not actually writing—and I was afraid that with someone else around, I'd lose valuable thinking time. But family life has given me a sense of stability [that] has improved my writing rather than hindered it."[9] It helps, too, that both Carla and Sherre recognize Sachar's needs and are more than willing to make adjustments.

A Writer's Life

Like any writer, Sachar has his own way to deal with problems that occur. "It's difficult to say where ideas for stories come from," he explains. "I brainstorm until one idea leads to another which leads to another, and often it is the third or fourth idea which proves salvageable [able to be saved]. I've started books, worked on them for a couple of weeks, and then abandoned the story for another. Through my first drafts, I never know what's going to happen, making the story terribly disorganized and subject to re-writes."[10] Sometimes writing itself is difficult, he says, "especially when I can't figure out what to write. Usually when I finish the book I look back and think it was fun to write, but while I'm writing it, it's not really fun at all."[11] The amount of time it takes Sachar to write a book varies from project to project. For example, books in the Marvin Redpost series can take anywhere from four to six months to complete, while Sachar spent more than eighteen months writing *Holes*.

Almost every new project begins the same way. Sachar spends about a month brainstorming before he begins to sketch out ideas for characters and a plot. His early efforts, though, are often premature, leading to many false starts and dead ends. As he explained in his Newbery speech, "I'll get an idea, write a few words on my computer, think 'That's stupid!' and delete it. I'll try something else—'That's dumb!'—and try again."[12] Sometimes, though, the process works in reverse, and Sachar returns to ideas he discarded earlier. "I'll get an idea that may not seem very special at first; however, as I write, it immediately starts to grow. One idea leads to another idea, and that idea leads to another idea . . . until I have a story going."[13]

Like many writers, Sachar often battles writer's block. Usually he will force himself to write anything in order to get through it. Because he does on average anywhere from four to six drafts of a book, he can work through any technical problems. When he is satisfied that he has an acceptable manuscript, he sends a copy to his publisher (Sachar has had different publishers for his books), but at that point the manuscript is far from done. Sachar works with his editor to revise it, which usually means Sachar will do additional drafts before the manuscript is ready for publication.

When it comes to discussing his own books and future projects, Sachar is quite thoughtful. He views his books on the Wayside School as "complete fantasy"[14] and believes that it is far more difficult to write realistic works such as *There's a Boy in the Girls' Bathroom*. When asked about the differences, Sachar replies, "When you write something like *Sideways Stories* people tend to say, 'What an imagination it takes to think of all those fantastical things.' On the contrary, I think it takes a greater imagination to write realistic stories complete with realistic details. It's simple to invent, but to get to the heart of reality takes some real creativity."[15]

One thing he does not think about when writing is the moral or lesson to be learned in his books. In his Newbery Medal acceptance speech, he stated, "It's hard to imagine anyone asking an author of an adult novel what morals or lessons he or she was trying to teach the reader. But there is a perception that if you write for young people, then the book should be a lesson of some sort, a learning experience, a step toward something else."[16] Sachar just wants kids to enjoy reading and perhaps to begin thinking about who they are and who they want to become.

It's important for writers to be aware of what others are doing in their field, and Sachar counts Katherine Paterson, Lois Lowry, Avi, and Walter Dean Myers as some of his favorite writers for young readers. He would like to try his hand at other types of stories, especially scary stories. Since completing *Holes*, he has written three more books in the Marvin Redpost series and has also adapted two of his books, *There's a Boy in the Girls' Bathroom* and *Holes*, for the stage. Sachar enjoyed this challenge because it gave him the opportunity to try something different. He also liked doing the adaptations because they added a new dimension to his work, allowing his characters to have a life of their own. But adapting a book to the stage proved more difficult than writing another book because, as Sachar says, it was "hard to generate the [creative] spark again."[17]

Louis Sachar works hard to keep his life in balance. When he is not writing, he takes long walks with his dogs, often in the company of Carla and Sherre. The whole family also volunteers weekly at the Austin Society for the Prevention of Cruelty to Animals (SPCA), where they help take care of homeless dogs. Sachar enjoys skiing and tennis, but he reserves his greatest passion for bridge. He enjoys the mathematical aspect of the game and participates in duplicate bridge tournaments all across the country. He has even earned the title of "life master" for his expertise at the game.

Still as passionate about writing for young people as he was when he first started more than twenty years ago, Louis Sachar, according to his daughter, sees himself as two different people: "a writer and a dad who just happens to have the exact same name."[18] Sachar's own quirky personality has provided him with one of the most important and interesting themes of his work.

When asked what advice he has for young writers, Sachar replies, "Read, find out what you like to read, and try to figure out what it is about it that makes you like it."[19] In his opinion, writing for children is one of the toughest but most rewarding occupations a person can undertake. As for the secret of his own success, Sachar says, "I try to think of the world as a kid would see it. Then I write a story that I would like as an adult."[20]

Interview with Louis Sachar

MEG GREENE: In your acceptance speech for the Newbery Medal, you mentioned the influence that your brother, Andy, has had on you. What was your relationship like when the two of you were growing up, and how exactly did he influence your decision to become a writer?

LOUIS SACHAR: I always looked up to my older brother. We were good friends, and I feel I learned my sense of the world more from him than from my parents.

MEG GREENE: How did you feel about moving to California? How did you like living there?

LOUIS SACHAR: Even though I had good friends in New York, I don't remember feeling any sense of regret over the move. Throughout my life, it's always been easy for me to leave the past behind and go on to something new. I liked being close to the beach and Disneyland.

MEG GREENE: What authors did you enjoy reading as a kid? Do they continue to influence your writing today? What have been some of the most important and enduring influences on your writing?

LOUIS SACHAR: I liked E. B. White, and I still do. I don't remember caring too much about books or authors when I was young. It wasn't until high school that I really started loving to read. The authors that influenced me the most were J. D. Salinger and Kurt Vonnegut. I feel like they continue to influence me, but I'm not sure I can say exactly in what way. I can just sometimes feel it when I'm writing.

MEG GREENE: What was your attitude about children before you began working as a teacher's aide? Did that change as you began to work more closely with kids?

LOUIS SACHAR: I didn't think much about kids. I was a twenty-two-year-old college student and was completely caught up in that world. I signed up to become a teacher's aide because it was an easy way to get college credit. I was a little concerned that I wouldn't be able to relate to them. Once I started, I was amazed by how much I liked all the kids. They were so much happier and more open than people my age.

MEG GREENE: Many adults believe that preteens and young adults are becoming too sophisticated and that YA writers must work harder to reach their audiences. Do you think children's authors, particularly those who write for young adults, have a tougher time reaching their target audiences? If so, why, and what ought writers do to rectify the situation?

LOUIS SACHAR: I don't think young adults have changed that much. Because of computers and video games, they may have a shorter attention span than in the past, but so do I. It's always been a challenge to write a good book that really moves a reader, and it will continue to be so. Writing isn't easy, and it never has been.

MEG GREENE: What made you decide to bring back Gary "Goon" Boone as a main character in *Dogs Don't Tell Jokes* as opposed to some of the other characters about whom you've written?

LOUIS SACHAR: *Someday Angeline* was my third book. I loved the characters I created, but I think the story could have been better. So I decided to give the characters another chance, this time in *Dogs Don't Tell Jokes*. I've had a harder time trying to write another story about Bradley from *There's a Boy in the Girls' Bathroom* or Stanley from *Holes* because they have already lived through interesting and complete stories.

MEG GREENE: One reviewer has called the characters in your books "empathetic misfits." How much do those characters reflect you when you were that age? Were you a class clown, a klutz, or the kid whom bullies picked on? Is there something more universal and less personal about your characters? Do you try to convey in your stories that almost all kids feel awkward, out of place, and perhaps a little frightened?

LOUIS SACHAR: Personally, I could always identify [more] with the antihero than with the James Bond type, and I think most people are that way. Kids, especially, feel that everyone else has it all together, and that they're the only ones who feel like an outsider. And there is a lot more satisfaction when a misfit succeeds.

MEG GREENE: In *The Boy Who Lost His Face,* you incorporated more mature themes and language. What made you decide to write for this age group? Do you prefer to write for younger or older readers?

LOUIS SACHAR: I've enjoyed writing for different ages.

MEG GREENE: The main characters in your books are both male and female. How difficult is it for you to write from a girl's point of view? Are there enough similarities between boys' and girls' perspectives that it is easy to make the switch?

LOUIS SACHAR: For the most part, I think there are enough similarities especially when they are young. I probably would have a more difficult time writing about older girls.

MEG GREENE: What made you decide to become a lawyer? What kind of law were you practicing?

LOUIS SACHAR: I never had a great desire to become a lawyer. I did well in school, and it seemed like a logical career choice. I didn't know if I'd ever be able to earn a living as an author. I ended up doing very little work as a lawyer, as I preferred to keep on writing.

MEG GREENE: The search for identity and learning to become more accepting of one's self and of others is a prevalent theme in your books. Is that something that you wrestled with growing up?

LOUIS SACHAR: Yes. As mentioned earlier, I think a lot of young teenagers feel inadequate and like outsiders. I hope my books will help them feel better about themselves.

MEG GREENE: Besides your books, you've done two stage adaptations and a screenplay. How did writing for the stage and film compare with writing a book? Was it harder? Easier?

LOUIS SACHAR: Writing novels is a very solitary experience. I never talk about my books with anyone, not even my wife, until I finish writing it, which may take a year and a half. Writing for the stage, and especially for the movie, was collaborative. A lot of people added their talents and ideas to the work. I enjoyed getting to work with very smart and talented people, but the downside was that other people made choices different from what I would have chosen.

MEG GREENE: Do you read reviews of your books?

LOUIS SACHAR: Yes. I'm curious about what others think of my work. Sometimes reviewers can analyze my work better than I can. I work on instinct. Things just feel right. A good review often articulates why what I did felt right.

MEG GREENE: What made you become more interested in reading when you were in high school?

LOUIS SACHAR: Good books.

MEG GREENE: You stated in an interview that one of the reasons you started to write for children was that you didn't like the literature available for kids. What didn't you like about children's books and what did you hope to do differently in your own writing?

LOUIS SACHAR: I found a lot of children's books to be patronizing and babyish. I try to relate to my readers as intelligent, creative, and thoughtful people.

Timeline

1954 Louis Sachar is born in East Meadow, New York, to Robert and Ruth Raybin Sachar.
1963 The Sachar family moves to Tustin, Orange County, California.
1972 Robert Sachar dies; Louis returns home from Antioch College.
1973 Sachar begins school at the University of California at Berkeley.
1975 Sachar begins working at Hillside Elementary School as a teacher's aide.
1976 Sachar graduates from Berkeley with a B.A. in economics.
1976–1977 Sachar works at Beldoch Industries, in Norwalk, Connecticut.
1978 *Sideways Stories from Wayside School* is published by Fillet; Sachar

begins law school at Hastings College of Law in San Francisco.

1980 Sachar graduates from Hastings College of Law.

1981–1984 Sachar practices law part-time in San Francisco.

1985 Sachar marries Carla Askew.

1987 *There's a Boy in the Girls' Bathroom* is published by Alfred A. Knopf.

1989 *The Boy Who Lost His Face* is published by Alfred A. Knopf; a daughter, Sherre, is born to Carla and Louis.

1991 Sachar and his family move to Austin, Texas.

1995 Sachar begins work on *Holes*.

1998 *Holes* is published by Farrar, Straus and Giroux. Sachar wins the National Book Award.

1999 Sachar wins the Newbery Medal for *Holes*.

2001 Sachar begins work on the screenplay for *Holes*.

2003 The movie release date for *Holes* is scheduled for April 18.

Selected Reviews from *School Library Journal*

The Boy Who Lost His Face
October 1989

Gr 5–7—The jacket art of a young man's horrified surprise as his pants fall down while he's talking to a girl in the school corridor captures much about the book, particularly its wit and humor (he's lost his pants, not his face) and its exploration of exaggerated situations that reveal the very real and excruciating angst of middle schoolers. David Ballinger fears being uncool, not fitting in, and wants so much to be popular that he helps some classmates attack an elderly woman and steal her cane. When odd things begin to happen to him, he believes the woman to be a witch who has cursed him, and his genuine remorse causes him to punish himself. By not being assertive, by not standing up for what he believes, he loses face. He grows in the course of the novel, and is able to get his "face" back, albeit somewhat bruised. Ample dialogue (including name calling, street language, and obscenities) and brief chapters will make this a book for which young patrons will reach. Unfortunately, the story is weakened by the tagged-on final chapter, set 150 years in the future, in which David Ballinger is revered, and his birthday has been made a school holiday. —Connie Tyrrell Burns, Mahoney Middle School, South Portland, Maine

Dogs Don't Tell Jokes
September 1991

Gr 5–8—Gary Boone (who calls himself "Goon") is the self-proclaimed clown of his seventh-grade class. He never stops joking, despite the fact that nobody laughs much, and he has no real friends at school. Entering a talent contest as a stand-up comedian forces him to look more closely at the effect his humor has on others and on himself. Sachar balances the fun with moments of insight and feeling. Gary, who appeared as a fifth grader in *Someday Angeline* (McKay, 1990), is not very funny as the book begins. He has moments of true wit, but they are overshadowed as he reels off one-liners culled from books. As he begins to notice how his family and classmates react to his jokes, he gradually becomes funnier. He also stops falling back on the self-deprecating humor that has helped to make him unpopular. His hilarious performance at the talent show is a fitting climax, full of real surprises. *Hurwitz's Class Clown* (Morrow, 1987) deals with a similar theme but is for a younger audience. *Dogs Don't Tell Jokes* is an excellent choice for junior high readers, and Sachar's younger fans will enjoy it, too. —Steven Engelfried, Pleasanton Library, California

Sixth Grade Secrets
September 1987

Gr 4–6—Laura's below-the-waist hair and her spirited personality have earned her a leadership role among classmates and the secret worship of Gabriel. She starts a secret club called "Pig City" and begins a covert chalkboard writing campaign featuring "pig" words. In an effort to win

Laura's attention, Gabriel sends a note, which jealous Sheila intercepts and changes. When Laura reads the now insulting letter, the battle begins. Eventually a rival club, Monkey Town, is formed. Warfare begins with silly pranks but soon escalates into ugly and destructive acts, culminating when Sheila and a friend sabotage Laura and cut her hair. The sheared Laura sees how foolish they've been, and the truth of Gabriel's affection comes to light. Laura's instant maturity may be a bit too rapid, given her stubbornness and intense pride, but overall, characters and their actions are realistic, uncomfortably so. The plot is predictable, and the writing style is just adequate, but the situations presented are on-target. The humor, frequent dialogue, and brief chapters make this suitable for reluctant readers. —Heide Piehler, Shorewood Public Library, Wisconsin

There's a Boy in the Girls' Bathroom
April 1987

Gr 4–7—An unlikely protagonist, Bradley Chalkers is a friendless, lying, insecure bully who is the oldest boy in his fifth-grade class. In this humorous novel that tells of Bradley's learning to like himself and to make friends,

Sachar ably captures both middle-grade angst and joy. Bradley's triumph comes through the friendship of a new boy at school and the help of the new school counselor. Readers, like the astute counselor, can see the strengths that Bradley has, and will cheer at his minor victories and cringe at his setbacks along the way. The story is unusual, witty, and satisfying, if not always believable: a few incidents just do not work. For instance, even though Bradley has not been doing his homework, his complete ignorance of it is unlikely ("He hadn't realized he would need to bring his book home"), and his total unfamiliarity with birthday parties is too extreme for a ten year old, even one who hadn't been to a party in three years. Yet Bradley's need for acceptance even as he holds back from classmates who might mock or hurt him is genuine, and his eventual success will gratify readers. —David Gale, *School Library Journal*

Selected reviews from *School Library Journal* reproduced with permission from *School Library Journal* copyright © 1987, 1989, 1991 by Cahners Business Information, a division of Reed Elsevier, Inc.

List of
Selected Works

The Boy Who Lost His Face. New York: Alfred A. Knopf, 1989.

Dogs Don't Tell Jokes. New York: Alfred A. Knopf, 1991.

Holes. New York: Farrar, Straus and Giroux, 1998.

Johnny's in the Basement. New York: Avon, 1981.

Marvin Redpost: Alone in His Teacher's House. Illustrated by Barbara Sullivan. New York: Random House, 1994.

Marvin Redpost: A Flying Birthday Cake. Illustrated by Barbara Sullivan. New York: Random House, 1999.

Marvin Redpost: Is He a Girl? Illustrated by Barbara Sullivan. New York: Random House, 1993.

Marvin Redpost: Kidnapped at Birth? Illustrated by Neal Hughes. Random House: New York, 1992.

Marvin Redpost: A Magic Crystal. Illustrated by Neal Hughes. Random House: New York, 2000.

Marvin Redpost: Why Pick on Me? Illustrated by Barbara Sullivan. New York: Random House, 1993.

Monkey Soup. Illustrated by Cat Bowman Smith. New York: Alfred A. Knopf, 1992.

More Sideways Arithmetic from Wayside School. New York: Scholastic, 1994.

Sideways Arithmetic from Wayside School. New York: Scholastic, 1989.

Sideways Stories from Wayside School. Illustrated by Dennis Hockerman. Chicago: Follett, 1978.

Sixth Grade Secrets. New York: Scholastic, 1987.

Someday Angeline. Illustrated by Barbara Samuels. New York: Avon, 1983.

There's a Boy in the Girls' Bathroom. New York: Alfred A. Knopf, 1987.

Wayside School Gets a Little Stranger. Illustrated by Joel Schick. New York: William Morrow & Company, 1995.

Wayside School Is Falling Down. Illustrated by Joel Schick. New York: Lothrop, 1989.

List of
Selected Awards

***Holes* (1998)**

Bulletin of the Center for Children's
    Books (1999)

The Horn Book Magazine, Fanfare List (1998)

National Book Award (1998)

Newbery Medal (1999)

Readers Choice Award for Teen
    Books (2002)

School Library Journal, Best
    Book of 1998

Voice of Youth Advocates Award (1998)

Sideways Stories from Wayside School (1978)

Children's Book Council (1979)

Children's Choice (1978)

Ethical Culture School Book Award (1978)

International Reading Association (1979)

There's a Boy in the Girls' Bathroom (1987)

Georgia Children's Book Award, University of Georgia College of Education (1987)

Iowa Children's Choice Award (1987)

Land of Enchantment Children's Book Award, New Mark Twain Award, Missouri Association of School Libraries (1987)

Mexico Library Association (1987)

Nevada Young Reader's Award (1987)

Parents' Choice Award, Parents' Choice Foundation (1987)

Texas Bluebonnet Award, Texas Library Association (1990)

Young Readers' Choice Award, Pacific Northwest Library Association (1990)

Wayside School Gets a Little Stranger **(1995)**
Garden State Children's Book Award (1998)
Golden Archer Award, nominee (1996–1997)

Wayside School Is Falling Down **(1989)**
Arizona Young Readers' Chapter Book
    Award (1993)
Parents' Choice Award (1989)

Glossary

alternative A choice between two or more possibilities.

bohemian A person who does not follow traditional behavior.

contempt Feeling that a person or thing is low or worthless.

deposition Spoken testimony that is transcribed on paper and is used as evidence in a court case.

diverse Different or made up of many kinds.

escalate To increase by stages.

faltering Losing confidence or purpose; hesitating.

flip Saucy or impertinent.

hindered Slowed down; delayed.

The Horn Book Magazine A critically acclaimed magazine established in 1924 that reviews and recommends the best new books published for children of all ages.

loopy Silly, ridiculous, or absurd.

magic realism Stories that combine everyday life with the fantastic or magical.

National Book Award The highest literary award that can be given to an American author.

Newbery Medal The highest award in American children's literature.

oblivious Unaware; lacking attention.

pedestrian Dull or uninspired.

premise Something upon which an argument is based or a conclusion that has been drawn.

prestigious Celebrated; important.

pun A play on words that involves similar sense or sounds of words.

ranting Speaking loudly or violently.

renounce To give up.

reprimand To scold.

Runyon, Damon (1884–1946) A New York journalist, sports columnist, and short-story writer best known for his 1932 story collection, *Guys and Dolls*.

salvageable Able to be recovered or reused.

sauntering Leisurely walking or strolling.

stigma A mark of shame or disgrace.

Texas Bluebonnet Award An award that honors children's authors, given yearly by the Texas Library Association.

villainous Wicked.

wry Funny in an ironic way.

For More Information

Web Sites

Due to the changing nature of Internet links, the Rosen Publishing Group, Inc., has developed an online list of Web sites related to the subject of this book. This site is updated regularly. Please use this link to access the list:

http://www.rosenlinks.com/lab/lsac

For Further Reading

Davis, Kate. "The *Holes* Story." *Read*, December 20, 2002, Vol. 52, No. 9, p. 12.

"*Holes*: The Movie." *Read*, December 20, 2002, Vol. 52, No. 9, p. 4.

"Interview: Louis Sachar and Sharon Creech Discuss Writing Books for Children." *Morning Edition* (National Public Radio), September 17, 2002.

"Paint a Picture for the Reader: A Conversation with Louis Sachar." *Writing*. November/December 2002 Teacher's Guide, Vol. 25, No. 3, p. 26.

Wingert, Pat. "Make Summer Count." *Newsweek*, June 14, 1999, Vol. 133, No. 24, pp. 77–78.

Bibliography

"Author Studies Homepage: Louis Sachar." *Scholastic Teachers*. Retrieved July 15, 2002 (http://www2.scholastic.com).

"Biographical Essay: Louis Sachar." Authors and Artists for Young Adults, Volume 35. Farmington Hills, MI: Gale Group, 2000. Reproduced in Biography Resource Center. Retrieved July 2002 (http://galenet.galegroup.com).

Bolle, Sonja. "On the Set of 'Holes.'" *Publishers Weekly*, July 22, 2002, Vol. 249, No. 29, p. 81.

Cooper, Ilene. Review of *Sixth Grade Secrets*. *Booklist*, November 1, 1987, p. 484.

Cooper, Ilene. Review of *Someday Angeline*. *Booklist*, September 1, 1983, p. 91.

Dingus, Anne. "Louis Sachar." *Texas Monthly*, September 1999, Vol. 27, No. 19, p. 121.

Follos, Alison. Review of *Holes*. *School Library Journal*, September 1998, p. 210.

Forman, Jack. Review of *Johnny's in the Basement*. *School Library Journal*, December 1981, p. 68.

Gale, David. Review of *There's a Boy in the Girls' Bathroom*. *School Library Journal*, April 1987, p. 103.

Hearne, Betsy. "He Didn't Do It." *New York Times*, November 15, 1998, p. 52.

Hearne, Betsy. Review of *There's a Boy in the Girls' Bathroom*. *Bulletin of the Center for Children's Books*, April 1987, p. 155.

Kornfeld, Matilda, and Lillian Gerhardt. Review of *Sideways Stories from Wayside School*. *School Library Journal*, September 1978, pp. 147–148.

Kowen, Kenneth E. Review of *Marvin Redpost: Kidnapped at Birth? School Library Journal*, March 1993, p. 186.

"Louis Sachar." *St. James Guide to Children's Writers*, 5th ed. St. James Press, 1999. Reproduced in Biography Resource Center. Farmington Hills, MI: Gale Group, 2002. Retrieved August 2002 (http://galenet.galegroup.com).

"Louis Sachar." *U.S. News & World Report*, February 15, 1999, Vol. 126, No. 6, p. 12.

"Louis Sachar." *U*X*L Junior DISCovering Authors.* U*X*L, 1998. Reproduced in Discovering Collection. Farmington Hills, MI: Gale Group. December 2000. Retrieved July 2002 (http://galenet.galegroup.com).

"Louis Sachar's Interview Transcript." Scholastic Teachers. Retrieved July 15, 2002 (http://www.scholastic.com).

McElmeel, Sharon. "An Award Winning Author: Louis Sachar." *Book Report*, January/February 2000, Vol. 8, No. 4, pp. 46–47.

"Meet the Author: Louis Sachar." Children's Book Council. June 30, 2002. Retrieved July 2002 (http://www.cbcbooks.org/html/louissachar.html).

Miller, Todd. "Keep on Digging." *American Theatre*, April 2002, Vol. 19, No. 4, p. 28.

Novelli, Joan. "Setting Takes You Places." *Instructor*, January 2001, Vol. 110, No. 5, p. 53.

Review of *Holes. Publishers Weekly*, June 27, 1998, p. 78.

Review of *Johnny's in the Basement. Publishers Weekly*, August 12, 1983, p. 67.

Review of *Sixth Grade Secrets. Publishers Weekly*, August 28, 1987, p. 80.

Review of *Someday Angeline. Publishers Weekly,* August 12, 1983, p. 67.

Review of *There's a Boy in the Girls' Bathroom. Kirkus Reviews,* February 1, 1987, p. 224.

Review of *Wayside School Gets a Little Stranger. Kirkus Reviews,* April 15, 1995, p. 562.

Sachar, Louis. Acceptance Speech. *Boston Globe*–Horn Book Award. Retrieved June 2002 (http://www.hbook.com/bghb_fiction.shtml).

Sachar, Louis. *The Boy Who Lost His Face.* New York: Alfred A. Knopf, 1989.

Sachar, Louis. *Dogs Don't Tell Jokes.* New York: Alfred A. Knopf, 1991.

Sachar, Louis. *Holes.* New York: Farrar, Straus and Giroux, 1998.

Sachar, Louis. *Johnny's in the Basement.* New York: Avon, 1981.

Sachar, Louis. "Louis Sachar, Newbery Medal Acceptance." *The Horn Book Magazine,* July 1999, Vol. 75, No. 4, p. 410.

Sachar, Louis. *Marvin Redpost: Alone in His Teacher's House.* New York: Random House, 1994.

Sachar, Louis. *Marvin Redpost: Is He a Girl?* New York: Random House, 1993.

Sachar, Louis. *Marvin Redpost: Kidnapped at*

Birth? New York: Random House, 1992.

Sachar, Louis. *Marvin Redpost: Why Pick on Me?* New York: Random House, 1993.

Sachar, Louis. *Sideways Arithmetic from Wayside School.* New York: Scholastic, 1989.

Sachar, Louis. *Sideways Stories from Wayside School.* Illustrated by Dennis Hockerman. Chicago: Follett, 1978.

Sachar, Louis. *Sixth Grade Secrets.* New York: Scholastic, 1987.

Sachar, Louis. *Someday Angeline.* Illustrated by Barbara Samuels. New York: Avon, 1983.

Sachar, Louis. *There's a Boy in the Girls' Bathroom.* New York: Alfred A. Knopf, 1987.

Sachar, Louis. *Wayside School Is Falling Down.* Illustrated by Joel Schick. New York: Lothrop, 1989.

Sachar, Sherre, and Carla Sachar. "Louis Sachar." *The Horn Book Magazine,* July/August 1999, Vol. 75, No. 4, pp. 418–422.

Stevenson, Deborah. Review of *Marvin Redpost: Why Pick on Me? Bulletin of the Center for Children's Books,* February 1993, pp. 167–168.

Stevenson, Deborah. Review of *Wayside School Gets a Little Stranger. Bulletin of the Center for Children's Books,* March 1995, p. 248.

Strickland, Barbara. "Louis Sachar: Top of His Class." *Austin Chronicle*, July 15, 2002. Retrieved July 2002 (http://www.austinchronicle.com/issues/vol18/issue26/books.sachar.html).

Sutton, Roger. Review of *Holes*. *Bulletin of the Center for Children's Books*, September/October, 1998, pp. 593–595.

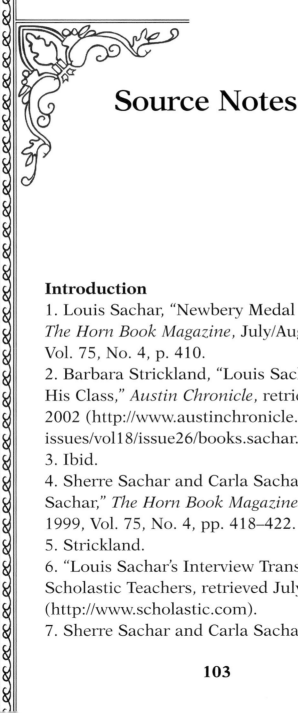

Source Notes

Introduction
1. Louis Sachar, "Newbery Medal Acceptance," *The Horn Book Magazine*, July/August 1999, Vol. 75, No. 4, p. 410.
2. Barbara Strickland, "Louis Sachar: Top of His Class," *Austin Chronicle*, retrieved July 15, 2002 (http://www.austinchronicle.com/issues/vol18/issue26/books.sachar.html).
3. Ibid.
4. Sherre Sachar and Carla Sachar, "Louis Sachar," *The Horn Book Magazine*, July/August 1999, Vol. 75, No. 4, pp. 418–422.
5. Strickland.
6. "Louis Sachar's Interview Transcript," Scholastic Teachers, retrieved July 15, 2002 (http://www.scholastic.com).
7. Sherre Sachar and Carla Sachar.

Chapter 1

1. "Louis Sachar," *U*X*L Junior DISCovering Authors* (U*X*L, 1998) Reproduced in Discovering Collection. (Farmington Hills, MI: Gale Group), December 2000, retrieved July 2002 (http://galenet.galegroup.com).

2. "Louis Sachar's Interview Transcript," Scholastic Teachers, retrieved July 15, 2002 (http://www.scholastic.com).

3. "Louis Sachar," U*X*L Junior DISCovering Authors.

4. "Louis Sachar's Interview Transcript."

5. Ibid.

6. Ibid.

7. "Louis Sachar," *U*X*L Junior DISCovering Authors*.

8. Ibid.

9. Ibid.

10. Ibid.

11. Ibid.

12. Ibid.

13. Ibid.

14. Barbara Strickland, "Louis Sachar: Top of His Class," *Austin Chronicle*, retrieved July 15, 2002 (http://www.austinchronicle.com/issues/vol18/issue2 6/books.sachar.html).

15. "Louis Sachar," *U*X*L Junior DISCovering Authors*.

16. "Louis Sachar's Interview Transcript."

17. "Biographical Essay: Louis Sachar," *Authors and Artists for Young Adults*, Vol. 35 (Gale Group,

2000), reproduced in Biography Resource Center
(Farmington Hills, MI: Gale Group, 2002), retrieved
July 2002 (http://galenet.galegroup.com).

18. "Louis Sachar," *U*X*L Junior DISCovering
Authors*.

19. Ibid.

Chapter 2

1. Anne Dingus, "Louis Sachar," *Texas Monthly*,
September 1999, Vol. 27, No. 19, p. 121.

2. "Louis Sachar's Interview Transcript," Scholastic
Teachers, retrieved July 15, 2002
(http://www.scholastic.com).

3. Dingus.

4. Ibid.

5. Sherre Sachar and Carla Sachar, "Louis Sachar,"
The Horn Book Magazine, July/August 1999, Vol. 75,
No. 4, pp. 418–422.

6. "Louis Sachar," *St. James Guide to Children's
Writers*, 5th ed. (Farmington Hills, MI:
St. James Press, 1999), retrieved July, 2002
(http://galenet.galegroup.com).

7. Louis Sachar, *There's a Boy in the Girls' Bathroom*
(New York: Random House, 1998), p. 3.

8. Ibid., p. 5.

9. "Louis Sachar's Interview Transcript."

10. Betsy Hearne, Review of *There's a Boy in the
Girls' Bathroom*, *Bulletin of the Center for Children's
Books*, April 1987, p. 155.

11. Review of *There's a Boy in the Girls' Bathroom*, *Kirkus Reviews*, February 1, 1987, p. 224.
12. David Gale, Review of *There's a Boy in the Girls' Bathroom*, *School Library Journal*, April 1987, p. 103.

Chapter 3
1. Louis Sachar, *The Boy Who Lost His Face* (New York: Alfred A. Knopf, 1989), p. 146.
2. Ibid.
3. "Louis Sachar," *U*X*L Junior DISCovering Authors* (U*X*L, 1998), reproduced in Discovering Collection (Farmington Hills, MI: Gale Group, December 2000), retrieved July 2002 (http://galenet.galegroup.com).
4. Louis Sachar, *Wayside School Is Falling Down* (New York: Avon Books, 1990), p. 172.
5. "Louis Sachar," *U*X*L Junior DISCovering Authors*.

Chapter 4
1. Sherre Sachar and Carla Sachar, "Louis Sachar," *The Horn Book Magazine*, July/August 1999, Vol. 75, No. 4, pp. 418–422.
2. Louis Sachar, "Newbery Medal Acceptance," *The Horn Book Magazine*, July/August 1999, Vol. 75, No. 4, p. 410.
3. Sherre Sachar and Carla Sachar.
4. Joan Novelli, "Setting Takes You Places," *Instructor*, January 2001, Vol. 110, No. 5, p. 53.
5. Louis Sachar, "Newbery Medal Acceptance."

6. "Louis Sachar's Interview Transcript," Scholastic Teachers, retrieved July 15, 2002 (http://www.scholastic.com).

7. Louis Sachar, "Newbery Medal Acceptance."

8. Louis Sachar, *Holes* (New York: Farrar, Strauss and Giroux, 1998), p. 5.

9. Ibid., p. 7.

10. Ibid., p. 27.

11. Barbara Strickland, "Louis Sachar: Top of His Class," *Austin Chronicle*, retrieved July 15, 2002 (http://www.austinchronicle.com/issues/vol18/issue26/books.sachar.html).

12. Ibid.

13. Ibid.

14. "Louis Sachar's Interview Transcript."

15. Review of *Holes*, *Publishers Weekly*, June 27, 1998, p. 78.

16. "Louis Sachar's Interview Transcript."

17. Strickland.

18. Louis Sachar, "Newbery Medal Acceptance."

19. "Louis Sachar's Interview Transcript."

20. Sharon McElmeel, "An Award Winning Author: Louis Sachar," *Book Report*, January/February 2000, Vol. 8, No. 4, pp. 46–47.

21. Ibid.

22. Sonja Bolle, "On the Set of 'Holes,'" *Publishers Weekly*, July 22, 2002, Vol. 249, No. 29, p. 81.

23. Ibid.

24. Ibid.

25. Strickland.

26. Louis Sachar, "Newbery Medal Acceptance."

27. Ibid.

Chapter 5

1. "Meet the Author: Louis Sachar," Children's Book Council, retrieved June 30, 2002 (http://www.cbcbooks.org/html/louissachar.html).

2. Ibid.

3. "Louis Sachar's Interview Transcript," Scholastic Teachers, retrieved July 15, 2002 (http://www.scholastic.com).

4. Ibid.

5. Sherre Sachar and Carla Sachar, "Louis Sachar," *The Horn Book Magazine*, July/August 1999, Vol. 75, No. 4, pp. 418–422.

6. "Louis Sachar," *U*X*L Junior DISCovering Authors* (U*X*L, 1998), reproduced in Discovering Collection (Farmington Hills, MI: Gale Group. December 2000), retrieved July 2002 (http://galenet.galegroup.com).

7. Sherre Sachar and Carla Sachar.

8. Ibid.

9. "Louis Sachar," *U*X*L Junior DISCovering Authors*.

10. Ibid.

11. "Louis Sachar's Interview Transcript."

12. Louis Sachar, "Newbery Medal Acceptance," *The Horn Book Magazine*, July 1999, Vol. 75, No. 4, p. 410.

13. Ibid.

14. "Louis Sachar," *U*X*L Junior DISCovering Authors.*

15. Ibid.

16. Louis Sachar, "Newbery Medal Acceptance."

17. Todd Miller, "Keep on Digging," *American Theatre*, April 2002, Vol. 19, No. 4, p. 28.

18. Sherre Sachar and Carla Sachar.

19. Louis Sachar, "Newbery Medal Acceptance."

20. "Louis Sachar," *U.S. News & World Report*, February 15, 1999, Vol. 126, No. 6, p. 12.

Index

About the Author

Meg Greene is a freelance author living
in Virginia.

Photo Credits

Cover, p. 2 © AP/Wide World Photos.

Design: Tahara Hasan; Editor: Annie Sommers